A to Z
Love Letters to You

ALISON MASSEY

ILLUSTRATED AND DESIGNED BY AAROHI BANSAL

Copyright © 2024 Alison Massey
Illustrations Copyright © 2024 Aarohi Bansal
Cover Design & Layout by Aarohi Bansal

All rights reserved. No part of this publication may be reproduced, distributed, transmitted in any form or by any means or stored in a database or retrieval system without the prior written permission of the copyright holder.

All inquiries should be directed to
www.flourishmyhealth.com

All Scripture quotations, unless otherwise indicated, are taken from the Holy Bible, New International Version®, NIV®. Copyright © 1973, 1978, 1984, 2011 by Biblica, Inc. ® Used by permission of Zondervan. All rights reserved worldwide. www.zondervan.com The "NIV" and "New International Version" are trademarks registered in the United States Patent and Trademark Office by Biblica, Inc. ®
ISBN: 979-8-218-55759-1

Dedication

To Kelsey and Caroline —

*May you always feel surrounded
by the love of God and your family.
Always cheering you on with
all my heart.*

- xoxo Mom

My Dearest

These are my love letters to you. You are a gift from God and I hope you will always remember how deeply God loves you. I'm grateful for the opportunity to care for you and to watch you grow.

My greatest wish is that you find

Love,

If I were an Astronaut I would fly to the moon and count all the miles to return to you.

When referring to heaven it's natural for us to look up at the beautiful vastness of the starry sky. Why is that I wonder? Perhaps, the celestial seems to be the visual evidence that best describes God's infinite wisdom and power. God created humans as caretakers for this beautiful earth. God cares about you. Your life here matters.

Psalm 8:3-4

"When I consider your heavens, the work of your fingers, the moon and the stars, which you have set in place, what is mankind that you are mindful of them, human beings that you care for them?"

This is what I remember about when I first met you:

_____
_____
_____
_____
_____
_____
_____
_____
_____
_____
_____
_____

B

If I were a Bird I'd soar in the sky, singing a tune waiting for your reply.

Throughout life you will hear so many unkind things, said about others and even directed at you. I hope my words as a parent, like those of a bird, are sweet and build you up. I might not always say the right thing at the right time, no parent does, but I hope you know it's always been my intent to be one that encourages you as you grow.

Ephesians 4:29

"Do not let any unwholesome talk come out of your mouths, but only what is helpful for building others up according to their needs, that it may benefit those who listen."

Watching you learn to talk and express yourself through words was so fun. These are some of my favorite memories of conversations that we shared when you were a child:

_____
_____
_____
_____
_____

The words and messages from God we read in the Bible serve as a guidepost on how we can deal with communication with others throughout our life. These are a few of the most important messages I've received that have shaped my faith:

_____
_____
_____
_____
_____

C

If I were a Chair I'd sit in place, waiting all day for your embrace.

Patience is one of the most difficult lessons to learn in life. Our difficulties start in childhood but can be something that we struggle with throughout our life, even as adults. It is no wonder that patience is considered one of the fruits of Spirit! We can look to God to grant us the patience we need and this patience can continue to grow just as our faith can grow throughout life.

Galatians 5:22-23

"But the fruit of the Spirit is love, joy, peace, forbearance, kindness, goodness, faithfulness, gentleness and self-control."

As your parent, this is what raising you has taught me about patience:

_____
_____
_____
_____
_____
_____
_____
_____
_____
_____
_____
_____
_____
_____
_____

D

If I were a Dragon, I'd use my fire to toast all the marshmallows you desire.

There are many dragons in this world that need slaying, things like injustice, racism, poverty, etc., and it can seem daunting at times to make this world a better place. Yet, good people in the world can provide a bit of light and sweetness. There is hope among the despair of this world. There is also hope in God's message to us. Never forget that bit of light that shines in this world, hope rises to the top.

Hebrews 11:1

"Now faith is confidence in what we hope for and assurance about what we do not see."

Hope isn't just a wish, from a spiritual sense it's a confident expectation of God's faithfulness. As a parent here are a few ways that I believe God has shown his faithfulness to us as a family:

_____

_____

_____

_____

_____

_____

_____

_____

_____

_____

_____

_____

_____

E

If I were Electricity, I'd be the spark to light up the times that seem so dark.

When you were little I felt that I could protect you from all the scary things in this world. As you grew and I had to send you out into the world more independently, I knew that I couldn't shield you from every hurt. I hope as your faith grows it will serve as your light for dark times you might face in your life.

2 Corinthians 4:6

"For God, who said, "Let light shine out of darkness," made his light shine in our hearts to give us the light of the knowledge of God's glory displayed in the face of Christ."

Children have a special way of providing those sparks of joy into everyday life. A few of my favorite memories of "joy moments" with you include:

_____
_____
_____
_____
_____
_____
_____
_____
_____
_____
_____
_____
_____
_____

F

If I were a Fairy I'd frolic all day, finding secret spots for us to play.

Childhood is brimming with moments of learning through play. There is so much joy and imagination in each activity. It is no wonder that Jesus had a special place in his heart for children. The Bible reminds us that we should maintain some of the wonderful and tender qualities that children naturally have as we walk in our faith journey.

Matthew 19:13-15

"Then people brought little children to Jesus for him to place his hands on them and pray for them. But the disciples rebuked them. Jesus said, "Let the little children come to me, and do not hinder them, for the kingdom of heaven belongs to such as these." When he had placed his hands on them, he went on from there."

These are a few of my favorite memories of playing with you and watching you learn about life:

_____

_____

_____

_____

_____

_____

_____

_____

_____

_____

_____

_____

_____

G

If I were a Garden I'd love each season, growing together would be the best reason.

Just like a garden, you grow and change so much each day. At times it seems like the growth is slow but small changes happen daily, even if it isn't obvious. Growth in faith can be much like a garden. There are weeds of doubt, worry and sin. Amongst the weeds faith, hope, and love can bloom and flourish from tender care. Growth is part of life and during my faith journey parenthood has been one of my favorite garden's of growth.

Matthew 13:31-32

*"He told them another parable:
"The kingdom of heaven is like
a mustard seed, which a man
took and planted in his field.
Though it is the smallest of all
seeds, yet when it grows,
it is the largest of garden plants
and becomes a tree, so that
the birds come and perch in its
branches."*

Just like a garden, there have been seasons of growth along with challenges during my faith journey. Here are a few stories about my faith during different seasons of my life:

_____
_____
_____
_____
_____
_____
_____
_____
_____
_____
_____
_____
_____
_____
_____

H

If I were a Hippo I'd wear a tutu, for spinning and twirling to entertain you.

Joy. Sweet joy. In childhood, joy can occur in the simplest of moments. It's precisely that happiness over something unanticipated at times that makes it so good. Joy is a fruit of the Spirit and gift from God for a reason; it's an enduring attitude of both the heart and spirit; an inner contentment and satisfaction despite external circumstances.

John 15:9-11

"As the Father has loved me, so have I loved you. Now remain in my love. If you keep my commands, you will remain in my love, just as I have kept my Father's commands and remain in his love. I have told you this so that my joy may be in you and that your joy may be complete."

Watching your joy explode during different moments as you are growing is one of my favorite things as a parent. These are a few of my favorite "joy moments" that I watched you experience:

_____
_____
_____
_____
_____
_____

The world is full of challenges at times but focusing on God, and his message to us, has helped me throughout my life. Here is how I've experienced God's joy in my life:

_____
_____
_____
_____
_____

I

If I were an Ice Skate I'd help you glide and twirl, to be a star of the figure skating world.

My role as a parent is to help support you throughout childhood so you can blossom not only physically, but spiritually, into the person you were created to be in this world. You don't have to perform or be a superstar to be fantastic in God's eyes, or mine. My hope is that over time you realize this, you are already wonderfully made.

Psalm 21:6

"Surely you have granted him unending blessings and made him glad with the joy of your presence."

These are some of the things that I learned as a parent watching you grow and shine your light in this world in your own way:

_____

_____

_____

_____

_____

_____

_____

_____

_____

_____

_____

_____

_____

_____

J

If I were a Judge I'd make sure all the rules left this world kinder and better for you.

Judgment is one area that many struggle with in this world. Judgment from others can be harsh and leave emotional scars that are slow to heal. The Bible teaches us that we should not cast judgment upon others but instead love others and leave the judging to God.

John 12:46-47

"I have come into the world as a light, so that no one who believes in me should stay in darkness. If anyone hears my words but does not keep them, I do not judge that person. For I did not come to judge the world, but to save the world."

As a parent, no one ever wants their child judged unfairly by others but hopes for their acceptance. While I can't control the judgment of others, this is my love letter on how I hope you handle the judgment you will face in this world:

_____
_____
_____
_____
_____
_____
_____
_____
_____
_____
_____
_____
_____

K

If I were a Kangaroo, I'd put you in my pouch, and make you giggle, bouncing all about.

Tucking you into a protective pouch in this world often seems like it would solve all my fears as a parent. Yet, the better strategy is to provide you with the right spiritual tools to be able to weather some of life's storms.

Hebrews 6:19

"We have this hope as an anchor for the soul, firm and secure. It enters the inner sanctuary behind the curtain,"

This is what I remember about what amused you the most as a child:

_____
_____
_____
_____
_____
_____

Here are a few of the spiritual tools that I hope to share with you to help you weather some of life's storms:

_____
_____
_____
_____
_____
_____

L

If I were a Lake I'd be wide, clear and blue—a place to watch sunsets and make memories with you.

Just like a sunset, the beauty of childhood appears and then sets for a new day, a new season of life. We have a short window to enjoy the beauty of childhood and create memories together. My wish is that most of those memories are filled to the brim with love, one of God's greatest gifts.

1 Corinthians 13:13

"And now these three remain: faith, hope and love. But the greatest of these is love."

This is what becoming your parent taught me about love:

_____
_____
_____
_____
_____
_____
_____
_____
_____
_____
_____
_____
_____
_____
_____

M

If I were a Mountain you could climb to my peak, look at the view and dream of other adventures to seek.

There are so many adventures that you will have during life's journey. Adventures that we will go on together as parent and child, and those adventures that you will have all on your own. Just remember that God will be with you on every adventure throughout life.

Psalm 90:2

"Before the mountains were born or you brought forth the whole world, from everlasting to everlasting you are God."

Some of the best adventures that we have had so far together include:

_____
_____
_____
_____
_____
_____
_____

Here are a few adventures I hope to have together in the future:

_____
_____
_____
_____
_____
_____
_____

N

***If I were a Notebook I'd save my pages for you,
to write your ideas and draw a picture or two.***

We often have dreams and ideas about life's journey. We might even come up with a plan to achieve those things and sometimes things work out differently than the story that we might write for ourselves. God reminds us that we don't need to worry about the blank unwritten pages of life's story. Each chapter will be unique and we can take lessons even from the chapters that turn out differently than how we may have written them.

Matthew 6:34

"Therefore do not worry about tomorrow, for tomorrow will worry about itself. Each day has enough trouble of its own."

Here is a story about something that happened in my life that turned out differently than expected and the lessons I learned from that experience:

_____
_____
_____
_____
_____
_____
_____
_____
_____
_____
_____
_____
_____
_____
_____
_____

O

If I were an Oatmeal cookie I'd be chewy and sweet, waiting on a plate as an after school treat.

The sweetest moments in life are often the simple moments. It's a giggle, a smile, a hug or holding a tiny hand in your own. In the Bible miraculous things happen in very ordinary moments and unassuming places. Jesus was born in a manger, very humble beginnings for the son of God. God doesn't need you to impress him with "the fancy" of this world, he cares about your heart. Remembering that message from God can free you to extend simple love to others; a smile, a hug, or even your favorite cookie.

Luke 2:7

"And she gave birth to her firstborn, a son. She wrapped him in cloths and placed him in a manger, because there was no guest room available for them."

This is one of my sweetest memories of a simple moment with you:

_____

_____

_____

_____

_____

_____

_____

_____

_____

_____

_____

_____

_____

_____

P

If I were a Prayer I'd be filled with words of grace, blessing your little, sweet, tender face.

Prayer is a conversation between you and God. Prayer can be simple or formal. Prayer can be practiced alone or with others. Prayer can be expressed out loud or done silently. Prayer can be so many things, done in so many different ways. Prayer is a time for not only talking to God but listening to him.

Jeremiah 29:12-13

"Then you will call on me and come and pray to me, and I will listen to you. You will seek me and find me when you seek me with all your heart."

These are some of the prayers or conversations I've had with God about you:

_____
_____
_____
_____
_____
_____
_____
_____
_____
_____
_____
_____
_____
_____

Q

If I were a Quilt I'd be handmade for you, with all the brightest colors to make the gray days less blue.

In Europe, some believe that quilting was first introduced by the Crusaders who wore quilted garments under their armor. Today quilting is thought of as a hobby and art. Quilts often display beautiful colors and elaborate designs that are often repetitive, create a pattern and provide unity and balance visually. The piecing together of scraps of fabric to create something beautiful and cohesive can be a metaphor for life. God can take the seemingly unrelated moments of our life, even the difficult ones, to mend together our hearts for a purpose.

John 14:27

"Peace I leave with you, my peace I give you. I do not give to you as the world gives. Do not let your hearts be troubled and do not be afraid."

If I were to create a quilt design to celebrate my faith this is how I would describe that design to you:

_____

_____

_____

_____

_____

_____

_____

_____

_____

_____

_____

_____

_____

_____

R

If I were a Road, I'd lead you home but also take you to the unknown.

Each person's faith journey is their own, a unique road traveled by that individual. Just like any journey, it's not always a smooth road, and life can have unexpected detours. God doesn't promise that having faith will make the road in life easy, or without trouble. He reminds us that he is present with us during life's struggles.

Psalm 46:1-3

"God is our refuge and strength, an ever-present help in trouble. Therefore we will not fear, though the earth give way and the mountains fall into the heart of the sea, though its waters roar and foam and the mountains quake with their surging."

Here is what I'd love to share with you about my faith journey and how it has shaped my life:

_____
_____
_____
_____
_____
_____
_____
_____
_____
_____
_____
_____
_____
_____
_____

S

If I were a Smile, I'd show up each day to send your bad moods far away.

The simple joy of a smile can brighten the mood of everyone, especially the smile of a child. While our moods change daily and even by the hour, never forget that God is constant, never changing, and always by your side regardless of the mood.

Proverbs 15:13

"A happy heart makes the face cheerful, but heartache crushes the spirit."

As a parent, these are a few memories that always make me smile:

_____
_____
_____
_____
_____
_____
_____
_____
_____
_____
_____
_____
_____
_____

T

If I were a Turtle I'd walk along with you, enjoying nature at the pace we want to.

Learning to slow down is one of the greatest gifts that children, especially smaller children can teach us as parents. Children aren't in a rush to be "on time" for anything, they simply enjoy being in the present. The Bible has many messages of the importance of focusing on the present. Finding peace in the present shouldn't be so difficult but in a world with so many distractions it can seem to be elusive at times. All those "may peace be with you's" in the church liturgy have a deep meaning, and aren't simply meant as a passing platitude. Focusing on God's presence in our lives can provide the peace of soul and mind we are seeking, allow us to find solace in every circumstance, and embrace the present in a more intentional way.

John 20:21-22

"Again Jesus said, "Peace be with you! As the Father has sent me, I am sending you." And with that he breathed on them and said, "Receive the Holy Spirit."

Finding peace in the present comes directly from God. These are the ways I've experienced reminders to slow down and seek his presence in parenthood:

_____

_____

_____

_____

_____

_____

_____

_____

_____

_____

_____

_____

_____

_____

_____

U

If I were an umbrella I'd shade you from each storm, keeping you dry, safe and warm.

Taking a walk with a young child after a rain shower might be one of life's most underrated joys. Young children spot a puddle and see all the fun in the jump, the resulting splash, and the muck on their boots. It's natural as parents to want to be that umbrella to protect our children. Yet, it's impossible to go through life, even childhood, without some disappointments, hurts and storms. Sheltering children from life's storms is important. After that storm passes, however, what might be even more critical is teaching about resilience–jumping into those resulting messy puddles that happen in life with a bit of joy. Faith in God is life's ultimate umbrella, not eliminating the storms but providing a strong handle to hold onto and assurance of finding peace in his presence, despite life's storms.

Hebrews 11:1-3

"Now faith is confidence in what we hope for and assurance about what we do not see. This is what the ancients were commended for. By faith we understand that the universe was formed at God's command, so that what is seen was not made out of what was visible."

This is how my faith has helped my resilience despite difficulties:

_____
_____
_____
_____
_____
_____
_____
_____
_____
_____
_____
_____
_____
_____

V

If I were a Valentine I'd run out of space, words of my love would be too hard to place.

Some of the greatest lessons we learn in life come about because of love. Human love is powerful but God's love is the ultimate love. God's love is unconditional and everlasting. The beauty of God's love is that we don't have to be perfect, earn it with good deeds or even specific actions. As parents we try to model God's perfect love to our children but our humanity oftentimes makes us fall short. The good news is that there is no need to strive to even measure up because God's love is perfect.

1 Corinthians 13:4-7

"Love is patient, love is kind. It does not envy, it does not boast, it is not proud. It does not dishonor others, it is not self-seeking, it is not easily angered, it keeps no record of wrongs. Love does not delight in evil but rejoices with the truth. It always protects, always trusts, always hopes, always perseveres."

This is how I can best describe how parenthood expanded my heart and capacity to love:

_____
_____
_____
_____
_____
_____
_____
_____
_____
_____
_____
_____
_____
_____

W

If I were a Wave rolling out at sea, I'd bring in the tides so you could play with me.

Storms or difficult times are a part of our experience in this life. God is there to help guide us throughout life's many challenges. As a parent, I want to protect you from the "storms" of life and allow you to enjoy the joy and play of childhood. Keeping you sheltered isn't always possible, but know that God guides us through each day.

Ecclesiastes 3:1

"There is a time for everything, and a season for every activity under the heavens:"

This is my prayer for you as you continue to grow and face life's many "storms" ahead:

_____
_____
_____
_____
_____
_____
_____
_____
_____
_____
_____
_____
_____
_____
_____

X

If I were a Xylophone I'd write a song, for you and your friends, to sing along.

Singing God's praises is part of worship. It's easy to give thanks, praise and sing when things in life are going well but during difficulties it can seem more challenging. Expressing trust in God and continued faithfulness will be a journey throughout your life but my hope is that you develop an understanding that God's love truly is "as high as the heavens and his faithfulness extends to the clouds." So, continue to sing sweet child and let your voice be heard.

Psalm 139:13-14

*"For you created my inmost being; you knit me together in my mother's womb.
I praise you because I am fearfully and wonderfully made; your works are wonderful, I know that full well."*

Music is such a wonderful art and expression of feelings and emotions. These are a few of my favorite songs and what they meant to me at certain points in my life:

_____
_____
_____
_____
_____
_____

Your favorite childhood songs include:

_____
_____
_____
_____
_____
_____

Y

If I were You, and you were me, we would laugh at the silliness of our family. You're the best you and I'm the best me. You are the only person that you should want to be.

Comparison is a true thief of joy. Children often compare toys or who got the larger scoop of ice cream. Unfortunately, comparison doesn't end in childhood but often continues into adulthood. We are all unique with different gifts and qualities that we can bring into this world.

Psalm 57:7-8

"My heart, O God, is steadfast,
my heart is steadfast; I will sing
and make music. Awake,
my soul! Awake, harp and lyre!
I will awaken the dawn."

There are so many qualities about you that are unique. These are a few of the qualities about you that I admire most and a few stories from childhood where I believe those qualities really stood out.

_____
_____
_____
_____
_____
_____
_____
_____
_____
_____
_____
_____
_____
_____

Z

If I were a Zed, I'd say, "read it again."
This alphabet love letter should never end.

God's love for you is never-ending. God is the ultimate perfect parent. I do my best as a parent but will fall short at times throughout your life. I hope you know, however, how much I will always love you.

Matthew 28:20

"And teaching them to obey everything I have commanded you. And surely I am with you always, to the very end of the age."

When it comes to love letters, the letters I write to you are some of my favorites. This is the last love letter in this book, but not my last love letter to you.

To My Dearest Child,
Please know that my love for you is hard to even put into words, but this is my best effort:

_____

_____

_____

_____

_____

_____

_____

_____

_____

_____

I hope you find the joy in these illustrations that I felt while creating them and you enjoyed interacting with them!

- Aarohi, Illustrator and Designer

www.ingramcontent.com/pod-product-compliance
Lightning Source LLC
Chambersburg PA
CBHW061359010526
44107CB00012B/996